# COOKING WITH HERBS & SPICES
## Christmas and the Winter Months

© Schwartz Spices,
Wenman Road, Thame,
Oxfordshire. OX9 3SL

Recipes: Gill Evans for the Schwartz Home Economics Division.

Photography: Paul Williams

Designed & Produced by:
Published Promotions (a division of RGM)
High Wycombe, Bucks.

For further information:
National Spice Information Bureau,
6, Cavendish Square, London W1M 9HA

SCHWARTZ SPICES ,
THAME, OXON.

# Contents

# Introduction

This is the third in the series of Cooking with Herbs and Spices by Schwartz. This new book contains recipes and hints to take you right through the winter months including all the festivities at Christmas. The recipes we have prepared for you are all new and produce exciting dishes with a difference. The recipes show you how a simple shake of Schwartz Herbs & Spices can transform your meals and add fun and excitement to cooking and eating.

Herbs and Spices have always had and always will have an air of magic and mystery.

From the fabled and exotic spice islands to the rich sunny climate of the Mediterranean – Schwartz bring you the flavours from nearly every Continent of the world, which can now be found on the Schwartz stand in most supermarkets.

**The Schwartz Quality Difference.** Herbs & Spices vary enormously in quality. To achieve the best results in your cooking one needs to use the best Herbs & Spices and with Schwartz you certainly have the best. To start with our Herbs & Spices are the cream of the crop. We know where to seek the finest produce from the best growing areas of the world. Then all of the impurities – dust – twigs, stones, stalks are carefully sifted out. You would be surprised how much is thrown away. It would be undetected if it were left in but you would know the difference straightaway in your cooking. Having taken all that trouble we pack the Herbs & Spices in our familiar glass jars with screw top caps. These are used because glass is the best material to preserve freshness. Plastic is porous and cardboard is never completely airtight. Our refill packs are also flavour sealed but once opened the contents of the sachet should be transferred to a Schwartz glass jar.

# Special Schwartz Offer

For those of you who missed the first two in our series of cookery books – 'Main Course Meals' & 'The Christmas Season' – we now offer you the opportunity of buying these at a special price of 50p each inc. of p.&p. Simply send 50p Postal Order made payable to Published Promotions for each book together with your name and address plus which title/s you require to:

Schwartz Spices
Cookery Book Offer
P.O. Box 106
High Wycombe
Bucks

# Party Hints

A party during the festive season can mean anything from drinks with savouries to the full-blown Christmas dinner, and there can be few people who are not faced with the task of organising one or the other. With a little forethought and planning your party can be unforgettably enjoyable. On the following pages you'll find lots of ideas to give you inspiration for your party. But parties aren't just a success because of the food. We give you below some tips on how to organise all aspects of your party from the initial preparation to the timely close:

* Allow ample time for menu planning, taking into consideration the likes and dislikes of the guests you have invited. It's a good idea to get starters and puddings made the day before if you can, or better still prepare and freeze ahead until required. Take into account the nature of the food too – bite-sized food, easy to handle, is a must for the buffet-style party!

* If your party is a "grand do" for dozens rather than a simple one for four then consider disposable plates and napkins – there are many colourful designs to choose from and it certainly saves on the washing up!

* Although Christmas is the time to "eat, drink and be merry" remember to provide a good selection of soft drinks for your guests. Try tomato juice with a sprinkling of Seasoning Salt and Pepper, or a teetotal punch flavoured with Cinnamon and Cloves. A good cup of coffee – hot or iced, will win favour alongside the more potent cups, punches and alcoholic brews.

* It is often difficult to gauge appetites and to cater for large numbers. Make sure your food doesn't fizzle out by having a good reserve of herb or garlic bread to satisfy man-sized appetites. Use 4oz/113g unsalted butter with 1 teaspoon Garlic Salt or 2 teaspoons

Mixed Herbs for each French loaf. Wrap in foil, bake in a hot oven for 15-20 minutes and serve hot.

✷ Wine, if you're serving it, should be thought about early. White wine should be chilled in the refrigerator about 2 hours before required. Open red wine at least one hour before it's needed so that it can 'breathe.'

✷ Every table needs its centrepiece and a spectacular one can be made by frosting fruit – especially the more exotic kinds often readily available during the festive season. Dip whole fruit in beaten egg white then into spice-flavoured sugar (1 teaspoon to 2oz/57g) and leave to dry. Suitable spices include Ground Cinnamon, Nutmeg or Mixed Spice but mix and match for variety. Arrange when dry on a cake stand and decorate with baubles and tinsel.

✷ Unusual buffet sandwiches or tasty small canapés can make your reputation as a party giver especially if you flavour them with a savoury or sweet butter. Paprika, Chives, Herbs, Garlic and Cinnamon will all prove popular with fish, meat, poultry, game, cheese or shellfish sandwiches. Mix 1 teaspoon of the herb or spice chosen with 3oz/85g softened butter. The flavoured butter will keep in the refrigerator for up to 2 weeks and will also prove infinitely useful for adding to grilled meat, cooked vegetables and the sweet ones for spreading on cakes and teabreads.

✷ Mulled wines and cups are the traditional Christmas party favourites but you can lift any drink into the festive class by colourfully frosting the rim of the glass. Mix 1 teaspoon Ground Cinnamon, Nutmeg or Mixed Spice with 2oz/57g plain or tinted caster sugar. Dip the rim of the glass in a little egg white then dip in the sugar. Refrigerate until the sugar looks frosty and dry.

✷ First impressions really do count so greet your guests with some unusual savouries with their pre-dinner drinks. Dust piping hot home-made croûtons with Garlic Salt or Seasoning Salt. Try making a quick and easy dip to serve with crisp vegetables by flavouring cream or cottage cheese with mixed herbs or chives to taste.

# Sherry and Mincemeat Pudding

**4-6 SERVINGS**

**For the Pudding:**

2 *tbs (30ml) clear honey*
Approx ½ a 1*lb (454g) jar mincemeat*
4*oz (113g) caster sugar*
4 *oz (113g) soft margarine*
6 *oz (170g) self-raising flour*
1 *tsp Schwartz Ground Cinnamon*
1 *tsp Schwartz Ground Nutmeg*
2 *eggs – size 3*
2 *tbs (30ml) sweet sherry*

**For the Sauce:**

2*oz (57g) butter*
1*oz (28g) cornflour*
1*oz (28g) caster sugar*
¾ *pint (427ml) milk*
*Sweet sherry to taste*

Place the honey in a 2½ pint (1.42 litre) basin. Spread over the inside of basin with a knife. Press a thin coating of mincemeat over the honey to line the basin. Place all remaining pudding ingredients in a large bowl. Mix well until thoroughly combined. Spoon mixture into the prepared basin. Cover with greaseproof paper and a pudding cloth tied securely with string.

Steam over a low heat for 2 hours in a covered saucepan half-filled with boiling water. Top up water occasionally as necessary.

To make the sauce, melt butter in saucepan. Stir in cornflour followed by the sugar and milk. Bring to the boil, stirring. Add sherry to taste and cook for 1-2 minutes.

Turn the cooked pudding onto a warm plate, decorate with holly and serve with the sauce.

This pudding may be made in advance, stored in a refrigerator for up to 3 days and reheated by re-steaming, or frozen for up to 6 months.

# Cranberry Dream Dessert

**4-6 SERVINGS**

**Base:**
2 *oz (57g) butter*
4 *oz (113g) digestive biscuits – roughly
crushed*
1 *tsp Schwartz Ground Ginger*

**Filling:**
6 *oz (170g) full fat cream cheese*
3 *oz (85g) caster sugar*
1 *tbs powdered gelatine (dissolved
in 4 tbs (60ml) hot water and allowed
to cool slightly)*
½ *pint (285ml) double cream – lightly
whipped*
½ × 350g (12½oz) *jar Ocean Spray
Cranberry Sauce*

**Topping:** *(optional)*
½ × 350g (12½oz) *jar Ocean Spray
Cranberry Sauce*
¼ *pint (142ml) double cream – whipped*

Melt butter in a saucepan, stir in crushed biscuits and Ginger. Use to line the base of a greased loose-bottomed 7″ (175mm) tin.

Soften the cream cheese in a large bowl. Stir in caster sugar and prepared gelatine mixture, fold in the cream and Cranberry Sauce.

Spread the mixture on top of the biscuit crumb base and leave in a refrigerator until completely set.

Remove dessert from the tin and spread remaining Cranberry Sauce over the top and decorate with cream as desired.

This dessert may be stored for up to 2 days in a refrigerator or up to 2 months in a freezer.

# Quick & Easy Christmas Puddings

**6 SERVINGS**

4oz (113g) butter
2oz (57g) dark brown sugar
1 tbs (15ml) black treacle
6oz (170g) self-raising flour
1 tsp each Schwartz Ground Cinnamon
 and Nutmeg
2 eggs – size 3 – beaten
2 tbs (30ml) brandy
4 oz (113g) currants
4 oz (113g) sultanas
2oz (57g) mixed peel

Place butter, sugar, treacle, flour, Cinnamon, Nutmeg, eggs and brandy in a bowl and beat together until thoroughly mixed. Stir in currants, sultanas and mixed peel.

Divide the mixture between six thoroughly greased, ⅓ pint (190ml) capacity dariole moulds. Cover tightly with foil and steam for ¾ hour. When cooked turn the puddings out of the moulds and decorate with holly sprigs.

Serve with brandy butter, sauce or cream.

The pudding mixture may be cooked in one 2½ pint (1.42 litre) capacity pudding basin and steamed in the conventional way for 2 hours.

The cooked puddings may be stored in refrigerator for up to 3 days or in a freezer for up to 6 months.

# Ginger Snaps with Brandy Cream

**MAKES APPROXIMATELY 15 BISCUITS**

**For the biscuits:**

2oz (57g) butter
2oz (57g) caster sugar
2 level tbs (30ml) golden syrup
2oz (57g) plain flour
1 tsp Schwartz Ground Ginger
Lard for greasing

**Filling:**

Whip together
¼ pint (142ml) double cream
2 tbs (30ml) brandy

Preheat oven to 350°F/180°C, Gas Mark 4.

Melt butter, caster sugar and syrup in a saucepan over a low heat. Remove from heat and stir in sieved flour and Ginger. Allow the mixture to cool until the side of the pan can be touched comfortably.

Thoroughly grease 2 baking trays and the handles of 2 wooden spoons with lard.

Place heaped teaspoonfuls of the biscuit mixture at least 4″ (100mm) apart on one of the baking trays (maximum 4 to a tray). Cook in oven for approximately 5 minutes until the biscuits are bubbling and of an even golden colour. Remove from oven and allow to cool for a few minutes until the biscuit mixture is almost set.

Meanwhile place 4 more heaped teaspoonfuls of the mixture onto remaining baking tray and cook as before.

Quickly, but carefully, lift a cooling biscuit onto a wooden spoon handle and wrap around with the bubbled side of the biscuit uppermost. Allow to set. Repeat using another biscuit and second spoon. The first biscuit will have set hard and the handle may be removed, re-greased and used for the next biscuit. (If the biscuits become too hard to shape round the spoon handles, return to oven for a few seconds and soften again.)

Continue cooking and shaping the biscuits until all the mixture is used.

Fill cold biscuits with the prepared Brandy Cream.

The unfilled ginger snaps may be stored in an airtight container for up to 2 weeks or frozen for several months before use.

# Christmas Macaroons

**MAKES APPROX. 12**

*1 egg white – size 3*
*2 oz (57g) ground almonds*
*2 oz (57g) caster sugar*
*½ tsp Schwartz Ground Cinnamon*
*A few almond flakes*

Preheat oven to 350°F/180°C, Gas Mark 4.

Line 2 baking trays with rice paper. Whisk the egg white until stiff, fold the ground almonds, sugar and Cinnamon into the egg white. Place teaspoonfuls of the mixture onto the baking trays.

Decorate with split almonds and cook in oven for 15-20 minutes until firm to touch and crisp.

Remove from trays when cold and trim away the rice paper from macaroon edges before serving.

# Mint and Currant Shortbread

**MAKES 6-8 PIECES**

*2oz (57g) caster sugar*
*4oz (113g) butter*
*6oz (170g) plain flour*
*2 tsp Schwartz Mint*
*4oz (113g) currants*
*Caster sugar for dredging*

Preheat oven to 400°F/200°C, Gas Mark 6.

Cream sugar and butter together. Add flour a little at a time, mixing well between each addition, until all the flour has been incorporated. Stir in the Mint and currants, Knead the mixture to form a smooth dough and press into a greased 7″ (175mm) shortbread mould or sandwich tin. Cook in oven for 25 minutes until golden brown. Mark into 6-8 pieces while still hot and dredge with caster sugar when completely cold.

Especially delicious served as a mid-morning snack with coffee.

May be stored in an airtight container for up to one week or in a freezer for up to 6 months.

# Schwartz Chocolate Log

3 *eggs – size* 3
3*oz (85g) light brown sugar*
3*oz (85g) plain flour*
2 *tsp Schwartz Ground Cinnamon*
1 *tbs (15ml) warm water*

**Filling:**
8*oz (227g) butter*
1*lb (454g) icing sugar*
2*tbs cocoa powder*
2*tbs (30ml) milk*
A *little icing sugar for dusting*

Preheat oven to 375°F/190°C, Gas Mark 5.

Grease and line a 7″ × 11″ (175mm × 275mm) swiss roll tin with greaseproof paper.

Whisk eggs and sugar together until light and creamy and a spoonful of mixture, when lifted with the whisk, leaves a trail.

Sift flour and Cinnamon together and gently fold into the whisked mixture. Carefully fold in the water and pour the mixture into the prepared tin. Cook for 15-20 minutes until well risen and firm to touch.

While still hot, turn the cake onto a sheet of greaseproof paper.

Place another sheet of greaseproof paper over the cake and roll the cake up tightly.

Leave the cake rolled in the paper until completely cold.

Meanwhile to make the filling, cream butter, sifted icing sugar and cocoa powder together. Add milk and mix well. Carefully un-roll the cake and remove the paper. Spread a thin covering of the filling over the inside of the cake and re-roll.

Spread a very thin layer of filling onto the cake sides and pipe remaining filling to completely cover cake to form a "log" effect or simply spread all the remaining filling over the cake and fork over to form a pattern. Dust with icing sugar, decorate as desired with holly, robins, etc. and carefully transfer to a serving plate.

The cake with filling may be stored in an airtight container for up to 3 days or in a freezer for up to 2 months. Alternatively the cake and filling can be frozen separately.

# Spicy Meringue Gateâu

3 egg whites – size 3
6oz (170g) caster sugar
1½ tsp Schwartz Mixed Spice
1 tsp (5ml) Camp Chicory and Coffee
Essence

**Filling:**
1 × 1lb 13oz (851g) tin peach halves
in syrup
A few Schwartz Whole Cloves
A few glacé cherries
1 tsp arrowroot powder
1 tsp (5ml) Camp Chicory and Coffee
Essence
¼ pint (142ml) double cream – whipped

Preheat oven to 275°F/140°C, Gas Mark 1

Whisk egg whites in a large mixing bowl until stiff. Add half the sugar, the Mixed Spice and Camp Essence to the whites and whisk again until stiff, glossy and forms stiff peaks when lifted. Fold in remaining sugar.

Cover a baking sheet with rice paper and mark with a 9" (225mm) circle. Spread half of the meringue mixture to fill the circle. Spoon remaining mixture into a piping bag which has been fitted with a large star nozzle and pipe large whirls around the edge of the circle base.

Place in oven for 2 hours until the meringue is crisp and dry throughout.

Allow to cool completely. Drain the peaches, reserving juice. Pat the peach halves dry using a paper kitchen towel and arrange on the meringue base. Stud the peach halves with a few Whole Cloves to form a decorative effect and arrange a few halved cherries in between the peaches.

Blend the arrowroot powder in a small saucepan with ¼ pint (142ml) of the peach juice and 1tsp (5ml) Camp Chicory and Coffee Essence. Bring to the boil, stirring. Cool the glaze slightly before pouring carefully over the fruit to form a glaze.

Pipe whirls of whipped cream around the edge and serve immediately.

The unfilled, cooked meringue case may be stored for up to a week in an airtight container. Not suitable for freezing.

**NB:** The finished dessert is best eaten within a few hours of preparation as the meringue will soon become soft.

# Mandarin and Gingerbread Ring

6oz (170g) self raising flour
2 tsp Schwartz Ground Ginger
1 tsp Schwartz Mixed Spice
2oz (57g) sultanas
3oz (85g) butter
4oz (113g) golden syrup
2oz (57g) caster sugar
1 tbs thin-cut orange marmalade
6 tbs (90ml) milk
1 egg – size 3 – beaten

**Topping:**
11oz (312g) tin Mandarin oranges
4oz (113g) icing sugar

Preheat oven to 325°F/160°C, Gas Mark 3.

Thoroughly grease and flour a 9″ (225mm) ring mould cake tin.

Sieve flour, Ginger and Mixed Spice together into mixing bowl. Stir in the sultanas. Melt butter, syrup, sugar and marmalade in a pan over a low heat. Make a well in the centre of the dry ingredients and mix in the melted mixture. Stir in milk and beaten eggs. Pour mixture into the prepared tin and cook in the oven for ¾-1 hour until the cake is well risen and firm to touch.

Allow cake to cool slightly in the tin before easing the cake edges away from the side of the tin with a knife and turning out onto a cooling tray. Leave until cold.

Drain Mandarin oranges and reserve juice. Arrange the Mandarin segments around top of cake. Sift icing sugar into a bowl and mix with enough Mandarin juice to form a coating-consistency icing, which when poured over the oranges will coat the top of the Mandarins and run down sides of the cake forming a decorative effect. Allow icing to set before transferring to a serving plate.

The decorated cake may be stored in an airtight container for up to 1 week or the undecorated cake in a freezer for up to 4 months.

# Coffee and Ginger Creams

**MAKES APPROX. 40**

1 *egg white – size 3*
1 *tsp (5ml) Camp Chicory and Coffee Essence*
3 *teaspoons Schwartz Ground Ginger*
12oz *(340g) icing sugar*
3oz *(85g) plain cooking chocolate*
*Almond flakes for decoration (optional)*

Place egg white and Camp Essence into mixing bowl. Sieve Ginger and icing sugar together and stir into the egg white mixture until thoroughly combined working to form a stiff paste.

Shape paste on a surface dredged with icing sugar to form a long sausage shape measuring approx. 1" (25mm) in diameter. Cut off ¼" (6mm) pieces and shape slightly to make neat rounds, place on greaseproof paper and leave uncovered to dry for about 12 hours. Melt chocolate and dip ½ of each Ginger Cream into the chocolate.

Place on a cooling tray and decorate with almond flakes or nuts as desired and leave until the chocolate is set completely.

Remove the sweets carefully and place in paper sweet cases.

# Coconut Cinnamon Squares

**MAKES APPROX. 40 PIECES**

7oz *(198g) tin sweetened condensed milk*
8oz *(227g) icing sugar*
6oz *(170g) desiccated coconut*
2 *tsp Schwartz Ground Cinnamon*

Place condensed milk in a mixing bowl. Sieve icing sugar and stir into the milk. Add coconut and mix well. Divide paste into two halves. Press one half into a small baking tin lined with greaseproof paper and greased well with butter. Add Cinnamon to remaining mixture and knead until thoroughly combined. Press on top of the unspiced layer. Place in refrigerator to set completely before cutting into squares and placing in sweet cases.

# Allspice Chocolate Truffles

**MAKES APPROX. 25**

8oz (227g) plain cooking chocolate
2oz (57g) butter
2 egg yolks – size 3
2 tsp Schwartz Ground Allspice
2 tbs (30ml) dark rum
Chocolate vermicelli
Glacé cherries for decoration

Melt chocolate and butter in a heatproof basin placed over a pan of hot water. Remove from the heat, stir in egg yolks, Allspice and rum. Mix well. Beat until mixture thickens. Place in a refrigerator until the mixture has hardened slightly. Shape the mixture into small balls and toss in the vermicelli to coat. Decorate with quartered glacé cherries and place in sweet cases.

# Spicy Fruit Fudge

**MAKES APPROX. 60 × 1" (25mm)**
**SQUARES OR 3 lbs (1.36 kg).**

4oz (113g) butter
½ pint (285ml) milk
2lb (910kg) granulated sugar
7oz (198g) tin sweetened condensed milk
1 tsp Schwartz Mixed Spice
6oz (170g) raisins

Place butter and milk in a large heavy saucepan, at least 7 pint (4 litre) capacity. Heat gently until butter has melted.

Add sugar. Stir over low heat until dissolved.

Stir in the condensed milk and slowly bring the mixture to the boil. Continue to boil rapidly, stirring constantly, for about 20 minutes until mixture begins to thicken and turns a caramel colour.

Remove from heat. Add Mixed Spice and raisins. Beat mixture vigorously for about 5 minutes or until it goes very thick.

Turn into a greased baking tin approx. 7" × 11" (175mm × 275mm). Place in refrigerator. Mark into squares before it gets completely cold.

# Grenada Light Fruit Cake

8oz (227g) butter
8oz (227g) caster sugar
2oz (57g) ground almonds
12oz (340g) self raising flour
3 tsp Schwartz Ground Mace
2 tsp Schwartz Ground Ginger
4 eggs – size 3
8oz (227g) dried apricots
8oz (227g) glacé cherries
15oz (425g) tin pineapple pieces

**Topping:**
2oz (57g) glacé cherries
4 tbs (60ml) apricot jam
2 tbs (30ml) water

Preheat oven to 300°F/150°C, Gas Mark 2.

Grease and line an 8½″ (212mm) loose-bottomed cake tin with a double layer of greaseproof paper.

Cream butter and sugar together until light and fluffy, stir in ground almonds. Sieve flour with the Mace and Ginger. Beat the eggs one at a time into the creamed mixture, adding a spoonful of the flour with each. Add remaining flour and mix well.

Finely chop the apricots, quarter the cherries and drain the pineapple pieces reserving the juice. Finely chop the pineapple pieces.

Carefully stir prepared fruit into the cake mixture until all ingredients are thoroughly combined. Spoon mixture into the cake tin. Hollow the centre slightly and cook in centre of preheated oven for 2½-3 hours until cake is firm to touch. (Cover top of cake tin with foil if cake browns too quickly during cooking.)

For the topping, arrange cherries in centre of the cake. To make a glaze combine the apricot jam and water in a small saucepan and bring to the boil. Strain glaze through a sieve to remove any large fruit pieces.

Brush the glaze over the cherries, top and sides of the cake.

This cake will keep for up to 2 weeks stored in an airtight container or frozen, without the cherry topping and glaze for up to 4 months.

The cake may also be marzipanned and iced in the traditional Christmas way.

# Spicy Date and Almond Fruit Cake

8oz (227g) butter
6oz (170g) dark brown sugar
3 tbs (45ml) black treacle
4 eggs – size 3 – beaten

*Sift together*
   12oz (340g) self raising flour
   2 tsp each Schwartz Ground Nutmeg,
     Cinnamon and Ginger

2oz (57g) blanched almonds – finely
   chopped
8oz (227g) pitted dates – roughly
   chopped
12oz (340g) sultanas
3 tbs (45ml) dark rum

Preheat oven to 300°F/150°C, Gas Mark 2. Grease and line an 8″ (200mm) square cake tin with a double layer of greaseproof paper.

Cream butter and sugar together. Stir in the treacle. Beat in the eggs one at a time, adding a spoonful of the flour and spice mixture with each one. Mix in remaining flour mixture followed by the almonds, dates, sultanas and rum. Hollow out the centre of the mixture slightly. Cook in oven at the pre-set temperature for approximately 2 hours or until the cake is risen and firm to touch.

The cake may be stored for up to 2 weeks in an airtight container or for up to 4 months in a freezer.

Decorate the cake in the conventional way using marzipan and royal icing, or serve simply dredged with caster sugar.

# Savoury Party Cones

**MAKES APPROX. 20**

*14oz (397g) packet puff pastry*
*Beaten egg for glazing*

**Filling:**
*8oz (227g) cooked turkey*
*4oz (113g) cooked ham*
*1oz (28g) margarine*
*1oz (28g) plain flour*
*½ pint (285ml) milk*
*2 tbs Schwartz Minced Onion*
*3 tsp Schwartz Salad Seasoning*
*Schwartz Paprika for garnish*
*Cucumber slices for garnish*

Preheat oven to 450°F/230°C, Gas Mark 8.

Roll pastry to a thickness of approximately 1/5″ (5mm) and cut into strips measuring 1″ (25mm) × 16″ (400mm).

Carefully wind a strip of pastry round a greased cream horn tin starting at the tip, winding round overlapping the pastry to just below the top rim. Place on baking tins, glaze with beaten egg and cook for approx 15 minutes until golden. Allow to cool a little before removing the tin from the pastry cones.

Meanwhile, to prepare the filling, finely chop turkey and ham. Melt margarine in a saucepan, stir in flour. Blend in milk. Add Minced Onion, Salad Seasoning, turkey and ham.

Bring to the boil, stirring and simmer for a few minutes until meat is thoroughly heated. Fill each cone with the sauce mixture. Sprinkle with Paprika and garnish with twists of cucumber.

Serve hot or cold.

The cooked pastry cones may be frozen for up to 6 months.

**NB:** If cream horn tins are unobtainable the pastry may be made into vol-au-vents to use with the filling.

# Mackerel and Dill Pâté

**4-6 SERVINGS**

*8oz (227g) smoked mackerel – skin and*
*  bones removed*
*3 tsp Schwartz Dill Weed*
*1 tsp (5ml) Borden Lemon Juice*
*¼ tsp Schwartz Ground White Pepper*
*¼ tsp Schwartz Garlic Salt*
*¼ pint (142ml) double cream – lightly*
*  whipped*
*1 egg white – stiffly beaten*
*Lemon and cucumber slices for garnish*

Place prepared fish in a bowl and add Dill Weed, Lemon Juice, White Pepper and Garlic Salt. Mash together well. Stir in cream followed by the beaten egg white.

Spoon into individual ramekin dishes, scallop shells or into one large bowl. Chill, preferably overnight. Garnish with slices of lemon and cucumber twisted together. Serve with hot toast or savoury crackers.

May be stored in a refrigerator for up to 2 days or frozen for up to one month.

# Special Creamy Potted Prawns

**4-6 SERVINGS**
*4oz (113g) butter*
*1lb (454g) shelled cooked prawns*
*2 tsp Schwartz Mixed Herbs*
*2 tsp Schwartz Onion Powder*
*Pinch Schwartz Cayenne Pepper*
*2 tbs (30ml) double cream*
*Lemon wedges and lettuce for garnish*

Melt butter in a saucepan. Stir in prawns, Mixed Herbs, Onion Powder and Cayenne Pepper. Fry gently for approximately 5 minutes. Remove from heat. Allow to cool slightly before stirring in the cream. Place in refrigerator until completely cold and the butter has set. Spoon onto scallop shells lined with lettuce. Alternatively, the mixture may be divided between ramekin dishes before the chilling stage.

Serve garnished with lemon wedges accompanied by hot toast, biscuits or crackers.

May be stored in refrigerator overnight. Do not freeze.

# Melon, Orange and Ginger Cocktail

**4-6 SERVINGS**

1 *tsp Schwartz Ground Ginger*
4*oz (113g) granulated sugar*
4 *tbs (60ml) water*
1 *large Honeydew melon – skin and seeds removed. Chopped into chunks or shaped into balls*
3 *large oranges – segmented, (all pith and peel removed)*
3 *Kiwi fruit – peeled and sliced (optional)*
1 *orange – sliced for garnish*

Place Ginger, sugar and water in a small saucepan and heat gently until sugar dissolved.

Boil for 5 minutes to form a syrup. Place syrup in refrigerator until completely cold. Meanwhile arrange prepared fruits in individual serving dishes. Pour the cold ginger syrup over the fruit. Chill before serving garnished with twists of sliced orange.

# Schwartz Carbonade of Beef

**4 SERVINGS**

2 *tbs (30ml) cooking oil*
1½ *lb (681g) stewing steak – trimmed and cubed*
8 *oz (227g) onions – peeled and sliced*
4 *oz (113g) celery – sliced*
1 *packet of Schwartz Spice'n'Easy Mix for Beef Casserole*
½ *pint (285ml) stout beer*
¼ *pint (142ml) boiling water*

**Topping** *(optional)*

4 *slices French bread each approx 3" (75mm) thick*
2 *oz (57g) Red Leicester cheese – grated and tossed in Schwartz Paprika*

Preheat oven to 350°F/180°C, Gas Mark 4. Fry stewing steak and prepared vegetables in the oil in a pan until the meat is browned and vegetables beginning to soften. Transfer to a casserole dish. Stir in contents of the Schwartz Spice'n' Easy packet, beer and water until all ingredients are thoroughly combined. Cover and cook for 2 hours or until the meat is tender.

Meanwhile cover the slices of French bread with cheese and Paprika.

Float the bread slices on top of the casserole at the end of the cooking time. Return dish to the oven for approx 5-10 minutes until the cheese is melted and bubbling over the bread. Serve immediately with green vegetables and creamed potatoes.

The casserole may be stored without the bread topping for up to 2 days in a refrigerator or for up to 2 months in a freezer.

# Winter Minced Beef & Vegetable Pie

**4-6 SERVINGS**

2 *tbs (30ml) cooking oil*
10oz *(284g) minced beef*
4oz *(113g) swede – peeled and finely chopped*
4oz *(113g) onions – peeled and sliced*
1½oz *(42g) plain flour*
14oz *(397g) tin tomatoes*
2 *tsp Schwartz Italian Seasoning*
½ *tsp Schwartz Garlic Granules*
¼ *tsp Schwartz Ground Black Pepper*
1 *tsp salt*
1 *beef stock cube*
12 oz *(340g) prepared shortcrust pastry*
*Beaten egg for glaze*
*Schwartz Sesame Seeds for garnish*
*Tomato slices (optional)*

Preheat oven to 400°F/200°C, Gas Mark 6.

Fry minced beef, swede and onions in cooking oil until meat is brown and vegetables are beginning to soften. Drain excess oil, stir in flour, tomatoes and juice, Italian Seasoning, Garlic Granules, Black Pepper, salt and crumbled stock cube. Bring to the boil, simmer for 5 minutes.

Meanwhile, roll out half the pastry and use to line a greased 8" (200mm) pie dish. Roll out remaining pastry to form a lid, pour in the prepared meat filling, brush edges with beaten egg. Cover with pastry lid. Seal edges and decorate as desired.

Brush pie surface with beaten egg and sprinkle liberally with Sesame Seeds.

Cook in oven for 30 minutes. Garnish with slices of tomatoes, or as desired.

# Sausage Marengo

## 4 SERVINGS

2 tbs (30ml) cooking oil
8oz (227g) onions – peeled and sliced
1lb (454g) thick pork sausages
½oz (14g) cornflour
14oz (397g) tin tomatoes
4oz (113g) mushrooms – wiped and sliced
12oz (340g) tin sweetcorn – drained
2 tbs (30ml) sweet sherry
3 tsp Schwartz Seasoning Salt
1 tsp Schwartz Marjoram
½ tsp Schwartz Thyme
¼ tsp Schwartz Ground Black Pepper
Cooked, shredded cabbage for garnish

Heat the oil in a large frying pan and fry the onions until soft and just beginning to colour. Drain and transfer to a plate. If necessary, add a little more oil to the pan and quickly fry the sausages until brown on all sides. Drain any excess oil. Return onions to the pan. Blend the cornflour with 2 tbs (30ml) of the tomato juice and add to the pan with remaining juice and tomatoes. Stir in all remaining ingredients except the cabbage. Bring to the boil, stirring, and simmer for 30 minutes, uncovered.

Place the sausages on a serving dish with a little of the sauce spooned over. Garnish edges of the plate with the cabbage and serve remaining sauce separately.

Serve with boiled potatoes.

This dish may be stored in a refrigerator for up to 2 days or in a freezer for up to 1 month.

# Tuna Plait

## 4-6 SERVINGS

2 ×8oz (227g) tins tuna fish in oil
3 sticks celery – thinly sliced
2oz (57g) red pepper – finely chopped (optional)
2 tbs (30ml) Mayonnaise
1 egg – size 3 – beaten
2 tsp Schwartz Lemon Pepper (or 2 tsp Schwartz Seasoning Salt)
2 tbs Schwartz Chives
14oz (397g) pkt puff pastry
A few Schwartz Poppy Seeds for topping
Green vegetables or salad garnish.

Preheat oven to 425°F/220°C, Gas Mark 7. Drain fish and discard oil. Place the fish in a bowl and add celery, red pepper, mayonnaise, half the beaten egg, Lemon Pepper (or Seasoning Salt) and Chives, mix carefully.

Roll out the pastry to an oblong measuring approx. 14″ × 12″ (350mm × 300mm). Transfer to a baking tray.

Spread the filling lengthwise down the centre third of the pastry. Cut horizontal, 1″ (25mm) width strips down each side of the pastry to within 1″ (25mm) of the filling. Fold the end pieces of pastry over filling and lift strips of pastry over the filling from alternate sides to form a plaited effect. Brush with remaining beaten egg. Sprinkle with Poppy Seeds and cook in oven for 25 minutes until golden.

Serve hot or cold garnished with green vegetables or salad stuffs as applicable.

May be stored in a refrigerator for up to 2 days or frozen for up to a month.

# Caribbean Iced Coffee

**MAKES ½ PINT (285ml)**

1 *tbs (15ml) Camp Chicory and Coffee Essence*
2 *tsp (10ml) dark rum*
½ *pint (285ml) ice cold milk*

**Topping (optional)**
1 *tbs (15ml) whipped cream*
*A little Schwartz Ground Cinnamon*
*or*
*Approximately 1 tbs vanilla ice cream*
*A little Camp Chicory and Coffee Essence*
2 *Schwartz Whole Cinnamon Sticks*

Pour Camp Essence and rum into a glass, add the milk and stir well until thoroughly combined.

Either top the drink with whipped cream and a sprinkling of Ground Cinnamon *or* with ice cream topped with a swirl of Camp Essence and 2 whole Cinnamon Sticks protruding.

# Apple and Blackcurrant Christmas Cup

**MAKES ½ PINT (285ml)**
½ pint (285ml) apple juice
2 Schwartz Whole Cloves
¼ of a Schwartz Cinnamon Stick
1 tbs (15ml) Blackcurrant cordial
Sugar to taste (optional)
1 apple – sliced, for garnish

Place apple juice, Cloves and roughly broken Cinnamon Stick in a saucepan and heat gently below boiling point for 5 minutes. Add blackcurrant cordial and sugar to taste, if required.

Place in refrigerator until completely cold.

Strain the liquid and discard spices. Pour into glasses and add slices of apple.

# Potent Party Punch

**MAKES APPROX. 2¼ PINTS (1.28 LITRES)**
1 standard sized bottle red wine
    (approx. 1¼ pints (712ml)
1 pint (570ml) medium sweet cider
3 tbs (45ml) honey (+ extra to taste
    if required)
3 tsp heaped Schwartz Whole Allspice
2 Schwartz Cinnamon Sticks – roughly
    broken
2 tbs (30ml) dark rum
Apple and orange slices for garnish

Place wine, cider, honey, Allspice and Cinnamon in a saucepan. Heat gently to just below boiling point for about 10 minutes.

Add the rum and adjust the sweetness to taste by adding a little more honey if required.

Strain the punch through a sieve, discarding the spices. Add slices of fruit for garnish and serve warm in warmed glasses.

# Loins of Pork with Herby Stuffing

**6-10 SERVINGS**

2 *loins of pork, each with approximately 6 chops. Ask your butcher for the loins, to be chined, scored and tops trimmed. This may need ordering in advance.*
8oz (227g) *fresh white breadcrumbs*
2oz (57g) *shredded suet*
3 *tsp Schwartz Herbes de Provence*
2 *tsp Schwartz Seasoning Salt*
1 *tsp Schwartz Ground Black Pepper*
15oz (425g) *tin pineapple rings*
1 *egg – size 3 – beaten*
*Cooking oil for roasting*
4 *Schwartz Whole Bay Leaves*
4 *Glacé cherries*
4 *cocktail sticks*
12 *cutlet frills*

Preheat oven to 400°F/200°C, Gas Mark 6.

To prepare the stuffing, place breadcrumbs, suet, Herbes de Provence, Seasoning Salt, Ground Black Pepper in a mixing bowl. Drain the pineapple rings and reserve the juice. Finely chop one of the rings and add to the stuffing mix along with 2 tbs (30ml) pineapple juice. Add the egg and mix with the stuffing mixture until all ingredients are thoroughly combined. Use the stuffing to stuff the joints as shown in the photograph and tie with string as necessary. Shape any remaining stuffing into small balls and cook around the joint for 20 minutes before end of cooking time. Cover the exposed bones with foil. Weigh the joint before placing in a roasting tin. Rub skin with oil and salt. Place a little oil around the joint in the tin, cover with foil and cook for approximately 30 minutes per pound (454g) plus 30 minutes extra, or until the meat is tender and juices run clear when the joint is pierced. To make skin crispy remove foil ½ an hour before end of cooking time (leave bones covered).

Place joint on a carving dish with stuffing balls, if any, and garnish as shown in the photograph using cocktail sticks to secure the fruit, where necessary.

Serve with green vegetables, roast potatoes, gravy and apple sauce. For extra stuffing, double the stuffing recipe quantities and shape into balls.

The cooked meat may be stored in a refrigerator for up to 2 days. Not suitable for freezing.

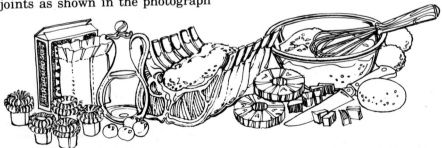

# Stuffed Duck with Orange and Cranberry Sauce

**4 SERVINGS**

1 *approximately 4lb (1.81kg) duck*
8oz *(227g) fresh white breadcrumbs*
2oz *(57g) shredded suet*
1 *tbs Schwartz Ground Coriander*
2 *tsp Schwartz Marjoram*
1 *tsp Schwartz Onion Salt*
¼ *tsp Schwartz Ground Black Pepper*
1 *orange*
1 *egg – size 3 – beaten*

**Sauce:**

½oz *(14g) cornflour*
½ *pint (285ml) fresh unsweetened*
  *orange juice*
9oz *(255g) Ocean Spray Cranberry*
  *Sauce – sugar to taste (optional)*
*Watercress and 2 cutlet frills for garnish*

Preheat oven to 375°F/190°C, Gas Mark 5.

To make the stuffing, combine breadcrumbs, suet, Coriander, Marjoram, Onion Salt and Pepper. Remove rind and juice from half the orange and add to the stuffing. Mix in the egg until all ingredients are thoroughly combined. Use to stuff the duck at the tail end. Sprinkle breast with salt and pepper. Weigh, place in a roasting tin with a little oil, cover with foil and cook for 30 minutes per pound (454g). If necessary remove foil ½ an hour before end of cooking time so that the skin becomes crisp and golden.

Meanwhile, to make the sauce, place cornflour in a small saucepan. Blend in orange juice, Cranberry Sauce and sugar if required. Bring to the boil, stirring.

Place duck on a carving dish, spoon over a little of the sauce and serve remainder separately. Garnish by arranging orange slices, cut from the remaining half orange, on top of the duck. Place cutlet frills on leg ends and watercress around the sides.

The cooked duck may be stored for up to 2 days in a refrigerator, and the meat, off the bone, for up to 1 month in a freezer.

# Minty Lamb and Redcurrant Chops

**4 SERVINGS**

8 *lamb cutlets or* 4 *lamb chump chops*
*A little cooking oil*
8oz (227g) onions – peeled and sliced
1oz (28g) plain flour
¾ pint (327ml) stock
2 tsp Schwartz Seasoning Salt
2 tsp Schwartz Mint
¼ tsp Schwartz Ground Black Pepper
3oz (85g) redcurrant jelly
8oz (227g) button mushrooms – wiped

Preheat oven to 350°F/180°C, Gas Mark 4.

Fry the lamb chops in a frying pan in a little cooking oil until brown on all sides. Transfer to a casserole dish. Fry onions in 2 tbs (30ml) cooking oil until soft and just beginning to colour. Stir in the flour. Blend in stock followed by all remaining ingredients except mushrooms. Bring to boil. Pour over chops. Cover and cook in oven for approximately 1½ hours or until meat is tender. Add the mushrooms 30 minutes before the end of cooking time.

Serve as desired, or as shown in photograph.

May be stored in refrigerator for up to 2 days, or for up to 1 month in a freezer.

# Spiced Brisket with Gravy and Herby Yorkshire Puddings

**6-8 SERVINGS**

1 × 4*lb (1.81kg) joint boned brisket (unrolled)*

**Marinade**

½ *pint (285ml) red cooking wine*
½ *tsp Schwartz Ground Black Pepper*
1 *tsp Schwartz Ground Allspice*
1 *tsp Schwartz Ground Ginger*
¼ *tsp Schwartz Minced Garlic*
1 *tsp Salt*
1 *Schwartz Bouquet Garni*
*Approx.* 12 *button onions – peeled*
8*oz (227g) carrots – peeled and sliced*
¾ *pint (427ml) Beef stock*
2*oz (57g) plain flour*

Prepare the marinade by combining wine, Pepper, Allspice, Ginger, Garlic, salt, Bouquet Garni and vegetables in a shallow dish.

Place the meat in the marinade, baste, cover and place in refrigerator overnight.

Next day, preheat oven to 325°F/160°C; Gas Mark 3. Remove meat from marinade and roll to form joint. Tie securely with string and weigh. Place in a roasting tin.

Add the beef stock to the marinade and pour over the meat. Cover with foil and cook for approx. 45 minutes per lb (454g) or until meat is tender. Baste occasionally.

When meat is cooked drain from the liquid. Carve into thin slices onto a serving plate, cover and keep warm.

Meanwhile, pour the cooking liquid into a measuring jug. Allow to stand for a few minutes so that the fat settles on the surface. Spoon 4 tbs (60ml) of fat into the roasting tin.

Blend the flour into the fat and cook over heat, stirring continuously until brown. Stir in approximately 1½ pints (855ml) of the stock according to the consistency desired. Boil for 2-3 minutes. Adjust seasoning to taste. Strain the onions and carrots from the gravy and arrange around the meat. Spoon a little gravy over, if desired and serve remainder separately.

**NOTE:** This meat is even more delicious if served with herby Yorkshire puddings made in the usual way but with 1 tsp Schwartz Mixed Herbs added to the batter before cooking.

The cooked meat may be stored for up to 2 days in a refrigerator or sliced for up to 1 month in a freezer.

# Gammon with Parsley and Mushroom Sauce

**4 SERVINGS**
*4 Gammon steaks*
*A little cooking oil*
*Grilled or baked tomatoes for garnish*
*(optional)*

**For the sauce:**
*2oz (57g) margarine*
*1oz (28g) plain flour*
*1 pint (570ml) milk*
*2 tbs Schwartz Parsley*
*2 tsp Schwartz Onion Powder*
*¼ tsp Schwartz Garlic Granules*
*¼ tsp Schwartz Ground White Pepper*
*2 tsp Schwartz Seasoning Salt*
*6oz (170g) Mushrooms – wiped and*
*sliced*

Brush Gammon steaks with cooking oil, snip rind edges at 1″ (25mm) intervals and either grill or cook in oven at 400°F/200°C; Gas Mark 6 for approximately 30 minutes or until the meat is tender, turning once during cooking. Grill or bake halved tomatoes for 5-10 minutes.

Meanwhile to make the sauce, melt the margarine in a saucepan, stir in the flour. Gradually add the milk followed by remaining ingredients. Bring to the boil stirring. Simmer gently for 5 minutes.

Arrange Gammon steaks on a serving plate. Cover each with a little sauce. Garnish with the cooked tomato halves. Serve remaining sauce separately.

Not suitable for reheating or freezing.

# Toasted Sandwich Ideas

## CHILI BEEF

*Bread and butter*
*Slices of corned beef*
*Schwartz Mild Chili Powder*
*Bick's Onion Relish*

Butter the bread and sandwich together with corned beef covered with a sprinkling of Mild Chili Powder to taste and Onion Relish. Toast under a hot grill on both sides.

## SPICY BACON & TOMATO

*Bread and butter*
*Cooked bacon rashers*
*Schwartz Grill Seasoning*
*Tomatoes*

Butter the bread and sandwich together with bacon rashers covered with a sprinkling of Grill Seasoning to taste and slices of tomato. Toast under a hot grill on both sides.

## HERBY MUSHROOM & PÂTÉ

*Bread and butter*
*Mild pâté*
*Schwartz Mixed Herbs*
*Schwartz Garlic Salt*
*Schwartz Ground Black Pepper*
*Fried sliced mushrooms*

Butter the bread and sandwich together with pâté covered with a sprinkling of Mixed Herbs, Garlic Salt and Black Pepper to taste and fried mushrooms. Toast under a hot grill on both sides.

## SPICY & FRUITY

*Bread and butter*
*Slices of banana*
*Schwartz Ground Cinnamon*

Butter the bread and sandwich together with slices of banana sprinkled with Ground Cinnamon to taste. Toast under a hot grill on both sides.

# Open Sandwiches

**Each filling makes enough for
4 servings**

## TURKEY TOPPER

*8oz (227g) cooked turkey – cut into
   small pieces
2 tbs (30ml) Mayonnaise
1 tbs Schwartz Parsley
1 tsp Schwartz Sandwich Seasoning
4 lettuce leaves – washed
4 slices brown bread – buttered
8 tomato slices, 16 small onion rings
A few Schwartz Sesame Seeds –
   toasted until golden.*

Combine turkey with mayonnaise,
Parsley and Sandwich Seasoning.
Chill for about an hour.

   Place a lettuce leaf on each slice
of bread. Cover each with some of
the turkey mixture.

   Arrange 2 tomato slices and 4
onion rings on each and sprinkle
the tomato slices with Sesame
Seeds.

## COTTAGE DELIGHT

*12oz (340g) cottage cheese
2 tsp Schwartz Salad Seasoning
2 tsp Schwartz Chives
8 dark crispbreads – buttered
8 lettuce leaves – washed
Walnut halves and segments of
   mandarin oranges or satsumas*

Combine cottage cheese with Salad
Seasoning and Chives. Allow to
chill for about an hour.

   Arrange the lettuce leaves on the
crispbreads. Cover each with some
of the cheese mixture. Garnish with
walnut halves and orange slices as
desired.

# Hot Mexicano Turkey

**4 SERVINGS**

1 *tbs (15ml) cooking oil*
8*oz (227g) onions – peeled and sliced*
12*oz (340g) cold cooked turkey – cut into chunks*
1 *packet Schwartz Spice'n'Easy Mix for Chili Con Carne*
14*oz (397g) tin tomatoes*
14*oz (397g) tin baked beans in tomato sauce*
¼ *pint (142ml) stock*
5 *fl oz (142ml) natural yogurt (optional)*

Using a large saucepan fry the onions in the oil until soft and just beginning to colour. Stir in all remaining ingredients except yogurt. Cover and simmer gently for 20 minutes.

If a less hot chili flavour is required stir in the yogurt in swirls at the end of cooking time.

Serve with jacket potatoes or crusty bread or other accompaniments as desired. Do not reheat this dish. Not suitable for freezing.

**Hint:** Cold cooked turkey may be sliced and frozen for up to 1 month.

# Schwartz Stir Fry Turkey

**4 SERVINGS**

4*oz (113g) butter*
15*oz (425g) tin pineapple pieces*
14*oz (397g) tin bean shoots or use 8oz (227g) fresh if available*
1 *each red and green pepper – deseeded and very thinly sliced*
4*oz (113g) mushrooms – wiped and thinly sliced*
4*oz (113g) celery – thinly sliced*
12*oz (340g) cooked turkey – cut into thin strips*
1 *tbs Schwartz Minced Onion*

**For the sauce:**

1*oz (28g) cornflour*
2 *tbs (30ml) soy sauce*
2 *tbs (30ml) clear honey*
½ *tsp Schwartz Ground Ginger*
¼ *tsp Schwartz Garlic Granules*
½ *tsp Schwartz Ground Black Pepper*
*Salt to taste*
*Toasted almond flakes for garnish*

Melt the butter over a low heat in a large frying pan or Wok. Drain pineapple pieces and reserve juice. If using tinned bean shoots drain and discard the liquid. Add pineapple pieces, bean shoots, peppers, mushrooms, celery, turkey and Minced Onion to the frying pan. Fry very quickly, stirring, for just long enough to heat the turkey.

Blend cornflour with the pineapple juice, soy sauce, clear honey, Ginger, Garlic and Black Pepper. Pour over the frying pan mixture and bring to the boil, stirring. Add salt to taste.

Serve immediately while the vegetables are still crisp and crunchy, garnished with toasted almond flakes. Serve with boiled rice or other accompaniments as desired.

This dish should not be reheated and is not suitable for freezing.

The vegetables and fruit used in the recipe are suggestions and may be varied according to personal taste.

# Turkey Curry with Mangoes

**4 SERVINGS**

2 tbs (30ml) cooking oil
8oz (227g) onions – peeled and sliced
2 tbs Schwartz Curry Powder – Mild,
  Medium, Hot or Extra Hot.
1oz (28g) plain flour
14oz (397g) tin of mangoes
Chicken stock
4oz (113g) raisins
½oz (14g) desiccated coconut
½ tsp salt
1lb (454g) cooked turkey – roughly
  chopped.

Heat the cooking oil in a large saucepan. Add the onions and fry until soft and just beginning to colour. Stir in Curry Powder and flour and fry gently for 1 minute. Drain the mangoes and make the juice up to 1¼ pints (712ml) with stock.

Stir into the saucepan followed by the raisins, coconut and salt. Bring to the boil stirring.

Stir in the turkey meat, taking care to keep the meat in whole pieces.

Cover and simmer for 30 minutes, adding the mango pieces 5 minutes before end of cooking time.

Serve with boiled rice and accompaniments as desired, eg. poppadums, chappaties, relishes, peppers, bananas, gherkins, melon etc.

Do not reheat this dish. Not suitable for freezing.

# Crispy Topped Sage and Sausage Bake

## 4 SERVINGS

*8oz (227g) onions – peeled and sliced*
*6oz (170g) carrots – peeled and sliced*
*1 large cooking apple – peeled cored and*
  *finely chopped*
*1oz (28g) plain flour*
*1 tbs Schwartz Paprika*
*1 tbs Schwartz Seasoning Salt*
*1lb (454g) pork sausagemeat*
  *(non-herby)*
*2 tsp Schwartz Sage*
*¼ tsp Schwartz Garlic Granules*
*¼ tsp Schwartz Ground Black Pepper*
*1lb (454g) potatoes – peeled and thinly*
  *sliced*
*A little oil for brushing and Schwartz*
  *Seasoning Salt for sprinkling*

Preheat oven to 400°F/200°C, Gas Mark 6.

Place prepared onions, carrots and apple in an approximately 3 pint (1.70 litres) casserole dish. Mix flour, Paprika and Seasoning Salt together. Add to the casserole and stir so that vegetables are well coated.

Combine sausagemeat with the Sage, Garlic Granules, Black Pepper and spread to form a layer covering the vegetables.

Arrange sliced potatoes on top to completely cover the sausagemeat. Brush with oil and sprinkle liberally with Seasoning Salt. Cook, uncovered, in oven for 1½ hours until the potatoes are cooked, crispy and golden brown.

This dish may be stored in a refrigerator for up to 2 days or frozen for up to 2 months.

# Bick's Turkey Burgers

**MAKES 8 BURGERS**

1 lb (454 g) cooked turkey – minced
3 tsp Schwartz Mixed Herbs
2 oz (57 g) plain flour
3 heaped tbs Bick's Hamburger Relish +
   other Bick's varieties for serving
Salt and pepper to taste
1 egg – size 3
Cooking oil for brushing
Bread baps
Lettuce

If using oven preheat to 400°F/
200°C, Gas Mark 6.

In a mixing bowl combine turkey, Mixed Herbs and flour. Stir in Hamburger Relish, salt and pepper and egg until all ingredients are thoroughly combined. Shape into 8 flat burgers. Place on a greased baking tray and brush with cooking oil. Cook for 25 minutes in oven or under a hot grill. Turn once during cooking and brush remaining side of burger with oil.

Serve in buttered baps with lettuce and other Bicks varieties.

Do not reheat the burgers. Not suitable for freezing.

# Savoury Leek & Rosemary Flan

**4-6 SERVINGS**

**For the pastry:**

1oz (28g) margarine
2oz (57g) lard
6oz (170g) plain flour
1 tsp Schwartz Seasoning Salt
1½ tsp Schwartz Rosemary
cold water for mixing

**Filling:**

8oz (227g) leeks – trimmed, washed and
    cut into approx. 2" (50mm) pieces.
1oz (28g) margarine
1oz (28g) plain flour
½ pint (285ml) milk
4oz (113g) mushrooms – wiped
    and sliced
½ tsp Schwartz Rosemary
1 tsp Schwartz Seasoning Salt
¼ tsp Schwartz Ground White Pepper
4oz (113g) Cheddar cheese – grated
3 hardboiled eggs – size 3
1 large tomato – sliced for garnish

Preheat oven to 400°F/200°C, Gas Mark 6.

Rub margarine and lard into the flour, stir in Seasoning Salt, Rosemary and enough cold water to form a soft dough. Roll pastry out on a floured surface and use to line a greased 8" (200mm) flan dish. Place a round of greased greaseproof paper slightly larger than the pastry case inside the pastry, greased side down. Half fill with uncooked dried beans or rice. Place in oven and cook for 15 minutes or until the pastry is set. Remove baking beans and paper, return to oven and cook for a further 10 minutes until pastry is crisp.

Meanwhile, to make the filling, cook the leeks in boiling salted water for 10 minutes, drain carefully, keeping the pieces intact and pat dry with a paper kitchen towel.

Meanwhile, melt the margarine in a saucepan, stir in the flour followed by the milk, mushrooms, Rosemary, Seasoning Salt and White Pepper. Bring to the boil, stirring, add cheese and cook over a low heat until melted. Reserve 6 pieces of leek for garnish and gently stir remainder into the sauce.

Slice hardboiled eggs and arrange in the base of pastry case. Pour over the sauce.

Decorate, using the remaining leeks and the tomato slices. Serve hot or cold. Not suitable for freezing, but may be stored in a refrigerator for up to 2 days.

# Cheesey Basil Soufflé

**4-6 SERVINGS**

*2oz (57g) butter*
*2oz (57g) plain flour*
*¹/₃ pint (190ml) milk*
*6 eggs – size 3 – separated*
*2 tsp Schwartz Basil*
*2 tbs Schwartz Onion Powder*
*½ tsp Schwartz Garlic Salt*
*4oz (113g) Cheddar cheese – grated*
*8oz (227g) cooked ham – very finely chopped*

Preheat oven to 375°F/190°C, Gas Mark 5.

Melt the butter in a saucepan. Stir in the flour and blend in milk. Allow to cool slightly before adding the egg yolks, Basil, Onion Powder, Garlic Salt, cheese and ham. Mix well. Grease a 2 pint (1.14 litre) soufflé dish. Whisk the egg whites until stiff and carefully fold into the saucepan mixture.

Pour into soufflé dish and cook in oven for 45 minutes to 1 hour or until well risen, golden and firm. Serve immediately with sauté potatoes and vegetables as desired.

Not suitable for freezing.

# Nest Egg Pie

**4 SERVINGS**

*2oz (57g) butter*
*8oz (227g) onion – sliced*
*2lb (910g) mashed potatoes*
*8oz (227g) Red Leicester cheese – grated*
*2 tsp Schwartz Dill Weed*
*2 tsp Schwartz Grill Seasoning*
*Approximately 4 tomatoes – sliced*
*4 eggs – size 3*
*4 rashers of bacon, de-rinded, halved*
*    and rolled*

Pre-heat oven to 400°F/200°C, Gas Mark 6. Melt the butter and fry the onions until soft and just beginning to colour. Stir into the potatoes. Add 6oz (170g) of cheese, Dill Weed and Grill Seasoning. Mix well. Grease a large, fairly shallow ovenproof dish and place a layer of sliced tomatoes to cover the bottom, reserving a few slices for garnishing the top. Cover with the potato mixture and spread until even. Make 4 fairly deep evenly spaced hollows. Break the eggs into the hollows. Arrange reserved tomato slices around the eggs and sprinkle with remaining cheese taking care not to drop any on the eggs.

Cook in oven for 35-40 minutes or until the eggs are set and cheese is golden. Cook the bacon rolls in the oven for 15 minutes and use to garnish the finished dish.

Not suitable for reheating or freezing.

# Herb and Spice Index

Allspice, Ground, 19, 36
Allspice, Whole, 31

Basil, 46
Bay Leaves, 32
Black Pepper, Ground, 27,28, 32, 34,35, 36, 38, 40, 43
Bouquet Garni, 36

Cayenne Pepper, 24
Chili Powder, Mild, 38
Chives, 7, 28, 39
Cinnamon, Ground, 6, 7, 8, 11, 13, 14, 18, 21, 30, 38
Cinnamon Sticks, 6, 30, 31
Cloves, Whole, 6,16, 31
Coriander, Ground, 34
Curry Powder, 42

Dill Weed, 22, 47

Garlic Granules, 7, 27, 37, 40, 43
Garlic, Minced, 36
Garlic Salt, 6, 7, 22, 38, 46
Ginger, Ground, 10, 12, 17, 18, 20, 21, 25, 36, 40
Grill Seasoning, 38, 47

Herbes De Provence, 32

Italian Seasoning, 27

Lemon Pepper, 28

Mace, Ground, 20
Marjoram, 28, 34
Mint, 13, 35
Mixed Herbs, 6, 24, 38, 44
Mixed Spice, 7, 16, 17, 19

Nutmeg, Ground, 7, 8, 11, 21,

Onion, Minced, 22, 40
Onion, Powder, 24, 37, 46
Onion Salt, 34

Paprika, 7, 22, 26, 43
Parsley, 37, 39
Poppy Seeds, 28

Rosemary, 45

Sage, 43
Salad Seasoning, 22, 39
Sandwich Seasoning, 39
Seasoning Salt, 6, 7, 28, 32, 35, 37, 43, 45
Sesame Seeds, 27, 39

Thyme, 28

White Pepper, Ground, 22, 37, 45

The herbs and spices listed on this page are just a selection from the many varieties to be found on the Schwartz stand at your local supermarket.

*For a taste of the world's finest spices*
**–Schwartz it.**